Terrific
Literature Activities

MOTIVATING PROJECTS AND STRATEGIES FOR READERS OF ALL LEARNING STYLES

25
Terrific
Literature Activities

MOTIVATING PROJECTS AND STRATEGIES FOR READERS OF ALL LEARNING STYLES

by Lori Licciardo-Musso

SCHOLASTIC
PROFESSIONAL BOOKS

New York • Toronto • London • Auckland • Sydney

Cover design by Vincent Ceci and Jaime Lucero
Cover art by Chris Reed
Interior design by Jaime Lucero for Grafica
Interior art by Teresa Anderko
Interior photographs by Lori Licciardo-Musso

ISBN # 0-590-59932-1
Copyright © 1996 by Lori Licciardo-Musso
All rights reserved.
Printed in the U.S.A.

12 11 10 9 8 7 6 5 4 3   7 8 9/9

Acknowledgments

This book would not have been possible without the love and support of my family and friends.

To SHARON FRITZ, my principal and friend, thank you for believing in me and encouraging me to new heights of success. You have opened doors and created opportunities that have made this step in my career a reality.

To TERRY HUIE, my vice-principal and friend, for your endless patience and devotion to my computer education. Thank you for always allowing me to lean on you and for your hours of effort to make this book come to life.

To my students, friends, and colleagues at TAYLOR MIDDLE SCHOOL and the MILLBRAE SCHOOL DISTRICT for your continued support and encouragement, especially LEO ALVAREZ.

To TERRY COOPER, Editor-in-Chief, Scholastic Professional Books, for believing in me and making a dream come true.

To my parents, BOB and AUDREY LICCIARDO who have always said, "Yes you can!"

Thank you for always making me feel I could do anything I set my mind to. Finally, to my husband DAVE, my daughters BRIANNA, DIANA, and the LITTLE MUSSO on the way. Thank you for your continued love and support. Without you, none of this would have been possible.

Table of Contents

Introduction

My Goals

I have always enjoyed escaping with a great mystery or medical thriller, traveling to intriguing places of the past through historical fiction, and relating to new ideas through thought-provoking poetry. Like many ardent readers, I have favorite authors: mine include Amy Tan, Robert Frost, Robin Cook, and Tom Clancy. I still remember fondly the first time I read Louisa May Alcott's *Little Women*. It was a joy.

I've always wanted to share that joy with my students; to help them take the same pleasure from reading as they do from watching television or playing video games. I therefore began to search for ways to bring literature to life for my students. I wanted to encourage them to become lifelong readers.

My search for ideas took me through a fellowship with the California Literature Project and the Northern California Writing Project. The California Literature Project is an organization committed to empowering teachers with the skills to provide students with a thinking, meaning-centered English/Language Arts curriculum that centers around quality literature. The project focuses on classroom instruction that will help students develop the ability to read and write well and to speak and listen intelligently.

My search also sent me to a fellowship with the Northern California Writing Project, to reading conferences, and to middle school conferences. What I learned from these organizations, as well as from the many excellent teachers I've met through the years, has molded a style that works for me and gets my students excited about literature.

Core Literature

Throughout this book I refer to "Core Literature." The term itself is used in my school district and is defined as follows:

Core Literature emphasizes the in-depth teaching of quality literature as a focus of the language arts program. Students read a variety of literature at different grade levels; for example, fiction, non-fiction, poetry, plays, etc. Literature is the core of the reading program and thus the title "Core Literature." Exposure to quality literature encourages the growth of students through examining their own thoughts, personalities and relationships with others.

The strategies in this book, geared for students from grades 4–8, are designed to help students become successful readers. I use them or have used them in my own classroom. I teach grades 6–8, and I am a trainer in Core Literature and

Process Writing of all teachers of grades 4–8 in my district.

At the beginning of the school year I always emphasize for my students what successful readers do (and I mention what poor readers do, too). The chart I develop with them appears below. My hope is that students will understand my reading goals (to help them become successful readers) with every activity that we undertake.

Successful Readers

- Read for comprehension
- Use fix-it strategies
- Use active questioning
- Read and reread for comprehension
- Understand that a story unfolds
- Imagine scenes
- Relate story events to own experiences
- Hypothesize about events
- Read to understand
- Enjoy reading
- Maintain running dialogue with text

Unsuccessful Readers

- Read to decode
- Often have problems with blockage
- Often have passive involvement
- Read only once
- Read for correct answers
- Often do not imagine scenes
- See little relationship between story and self
- Experience little anticipation of events
- Often read to please teacher
- May not enjoy reading
- Read word by word, interacting little with text

Book Organization

This book is divided into three sections.

Section One: "Into Activities"

The "into" activities are designed to get students excited and curious about what they are about to read, and to build students' background information. "Into" activities are presented prior to reading a novel. I suggest that you select one or two appropriate "into" activities per book.

Section Two: "Through Activities"

"Through" activities are used during the reading of a novel. The activities are used to promote comprehension and to develop critical thinking and an appreciation of language. You can select several "through" activities to help students navigate through the book.

Section Three: "Beyond Activities"

"Beyond" activities are used to celebrate and evaluate a piece of literature. "Beyond" activities encourage students to "go beyond," to relate events and feelings in the story to those in their own lives. "Beyond" activities are meant to spark continued interest in reading. You can select one or two activities appropriate to a piece of literature.

Grouping

Many of the ideas contained in this book require students to work in groups. There are several effective ways to organize your students. Here are the four that I rely on most:

Random Grouping   I use random grouping when a group will meet for a brief period of time and when the product students are creating is fairly easy. Random groups can be arranged by numbering students off ("One, two, three . . ." "All multiples of two stand here . . ."), or by placing students in groups based on various criteria: the kind of toothpaste they use, favorite colors, favorite animals, or the month in which they were born.

Geographic Grouping   I use geographic groups when students will be required to meet with their group outside of school. I organize the groups based on where students live or where their after-school caretaker is located. I try to arrange groups so that the members are within walking distance of each other.

Set Groups   The students in my classroom sit at tables of four, rather than individually in rows. Seated in clusters of four, they are ready to work cooperatively at a moment's notice. I try to balance groups heterogeneously, with a mixture of all types of students, academically and culturally.

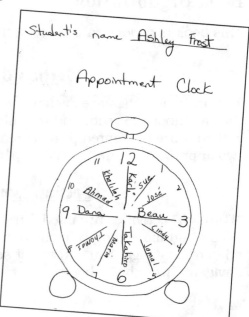

I change these groups four times a year, so that at various intervals students get acquainted with new students.

Pairs   When an activity is more suitable for pairs, I simply ask them to turn to the person seated next to them and consider that person their partner.

The "appointment clock" system is fun for a change of pace. It works this way: Students construct an appointment

clock on the first day of school. They fill the twelve spaces with classmates' names, according to the following criteria:

Students must get four different students to sign up on their clock. The criteria are as follows:

- Only one person can be a good friend.
- One person must be someone you hardly know at all.

For example, if Ashley has Beau sign the three o'clock space on Ashley's clock, then Ashley must sign Beau's three o'clock space. That way when you announce, "Your partner for today is your three o'clock appointment," those students end up as a pair. Students should keep their appointment clocks handy so they are available when you make announcements.

Literature Logs

Throughout this book I often refer to literature logs. The literature log is a written reflection of a student's thoughts, processes, discoveries, and writings as they travel through the novel. As the teacher, I direct students as to what I generally expect to find in the log.

What kinds of work do I find in students' notebooks? It is often students' responses from the "Into," "Through," and "Beyond" sections of this book.

The literature log can be a report folder, a three ring binder, a portfolio case, or other box or case that allows students to add or remove work easily.

Kathryn and Julia prepared a cover for their literature logs on *A Day No Pigs Would Die* and *The Vandemark Mummy*.

I have found that keeping a literature log well organized is crucial. I help students do this by asking them to keep a Table of Assignments. (See sample below.) This details the date and title of the assignment and whether or not the student has completed it. I keep a table of assignments at the front of the classroom the entire time we are reading a novel. It is great for students who are absent. Instead of asking, "What did we do yesterday?" students ask more pointed questions, such as "How do I complete the filmstrip for Chapter 5?"

Table of Assignments

Date	Assignment	Done
4/30	Mini Papers	✓
5/1	—Timeline 1800's	✓
	—Oklahoma / Maps	✓
	—Monkeys / Picture	✓
	—Cherokee Indians	✓
	—Sharecropping	✓
5/2	Relationship Web	✓
5/2	U.S. Map	✓
5/2	Quotes / Notes Ch. 2	✓
5/3	Ch. 2 Quiz	✓
5/3	Blast to the Past	✓
5/3	Colloquialisms	✓
5/5	Notes / Quotes Ch. 4	✓
6/7	Comic Strip Ch. 5	✓
5/8	Quiz Ch. 5	✓
5/8	Monkey Catching Booklet	✓
*5/9	Notes / Quotes Ch. 8	✓
5/10 – 5/14	How To Catch a Monkey	✓
5/13	Notes / Quotes Ch. 9	✓
5/14	Ch. 9 Quiz	✓
5/15	Quickwrite	✓
5/15	Wanted Poster	✓
5/15	Ch. 11 Notes / Quotes	✓

A Table of Assignments helps students keep organized and on track.

Time Allotments

I have estimated the amount of class time you will need to complete the suggested activities in this book. When I refer to a class period, I am thinking of a fifty-minute session.

I hope that you will enjoy this book and find many new ways to bring literature to life for your students.

Happy Reading!

Section One

"INTO" ACTIVITIES

ESTABLISHING PRIOR KNOWLEDGE

TIME ALLOTMENT:
Varies

LEARNING OBJECTIVES:
• Building Prior Knowledge
• Relating to students' own experiences

MATERIALS:
• *Vary*

Purpose

It is important to establish prior knowledge with students before they read a novel. Find out what students might already know about the history or circumstances of (a) character(s) in the novel. This helps students to either connect with the novel or to draw upon the knowledge that you have established as they read.

Activities to establish prior knowledge will be different for each book. Activities can range from simply presenting students with geographical and historical information to involving them in hands-on activities. Here are some effective hands-on experiences you might create for students.

If you are about to read a novel with your students where the character(s) is handicapped or living in conditions vastly different from their own, then think of ways that you might be able to simulate that experience for your students. It will help them relate to the character when they come to that part in the book as well as develop some prior knowledge about the condition or situation.

Here are some examples of projects in which I provided my students with active prior knowledge about a novel they were about to read. I hope these will stimulate exciting ideas of your own.

Sample Activities

In *The Cay,* the main character suddenly goes blind. As preparation for reading the novel, I blindfold my students for one class period. During that class period we go on a walk, do calisthenics, eat various types of foods (sour, sweet, spicy) and listen to a story. For homework, students write in their journals what the experience was like and how they would feel if they suddenly became visually challenged.

In the novel *A Day No Pigs Would Die* the main character grows up on a farm in the early 1900's. To help my students understand what that might be like, I ask them to give up all modern appliances (except the toilet) for three days. I ask my students and their parents to sign a letter or "contract" about the assignment.

I usually have students do this assignment on a Friday, Saturday, Sunday so as not to interfere with other homework that might need the computer. After the experience, I ask the students and their parents to write a joint paper on their reactions. They are to be honest about what they missed most and least.

Dear Parents:

We are reading a novel that takes place on a rural farm in the 1900's called A DAY NO PIGS WOULD DIE. To help students understand what life was like back then, I'm asking them to give up as many modern appliances (except the toilet) as possible for three days.

Students should keep a journal about their experiences. What was hard? What was easy? Did you break down and use an appliance? Why?

Parents do not have to participate but are asked to help their children stay true to the experiment. At the end of the experience, please help your child write a paper about their experience and hypothesize about what life would be like without modern conveniences.

Thank you for your cooperation and have fun!

Sincerly,

_____
Teacher's signature

_____
Parent's signature

_____
Student's signature

T I P

Activities like these are easy to create and stay with the students for a long time. They help students to relate to the novel and give them a greater understanding of the theme.

Parents are not asked to give up appliances unless they want to, but they are asked to help their children keep to their word.

They also hypothesize about what it would been like to have been brought up in a time where many conveniences were unavailable. How would their lives have been different? After this activity, students can really relate to Rob and his experiences.

Many excellent short stories and novels deal with what it is like to be a second language learner. (*Thank You, Jackie Robinson* is one that comes to mind.) A great exercise to help students understand what this is like is to ask your bilingual teacher or a parent who speaks another language fluently to come in and teach a simple lesson in their native language. Students quickly get the feel of what it is like not to understand the language, yet be expected to perform. Students are asked to write in their journals what this experience was like and how it will affect them in the future.

In *Tuck Everlasting*, a family accidentally drinks from a spring that gives them everlasting life. Prior to reading the novel, I ask students "If you could drink from the fountain of youth, would you? Why or why not?" I ask them to list the pros and cons of the situation. Prior to reading *Tuck Everlasting*, most of my students think life everlasting is a terrific idea. After reading the book, most have changed their minds. Doing this exercise prior to reading the novel helps students to develop a running dialogue with the text as they compare how they feel with what actually happens to the characters in the book.

HAVE YOU EVER?

TIME ALLOTMENT:
One class period

LEARNING OBJECTIVES:
- *Active questioning/running dialogue*
- *Anticipatory model (helping students compare their writing with that of the author as the novel unfolds)*

MATERIALS:
- *Pencil*
- *Paper*

Purpose

This is a quick, easy way to help students get ready to relate the events in a main character's life to those of their own. The questions you pose will be general enough to relate to your students but specific enough about the main character to get students excited about "meeting" the character.

Preparing the Activity

1. Create 8–10 "Have you ever?" questions that relate in some way to the main character in the novel. Questions should be general enough to be applicable to a wide variety of students, yet specific enough to touch on the life of the book's main character.

2. Type the questions on a half sheet of paper and distribute. Students can write responses on the other half of the sheet. Or place questions on an overhead projector and ask students to write responses on sheets of paper.

Doing the Activity

1. Review your "Have you ever?" sheet with your students. Students will choose two questions to respond to. Make sure that students know that they will have to share one of their responses in a small group.

Here are sample questions for *The Cay* by Theodore Taylor:

Have you ever...

- had to move away from a home you loved?
- been scared?
- judged someone by his/her looks?
- disobeyed your parents?
- had to say good-bye to a friend?
- been on a ship?
- been uncomfortable with someone you just met?
- had to depend on someone?
- had an incorrect first impression of someone?
- been superstitious?
- had a trusted friend?

---

2. Ask students to freewrite in response to the two questions of their choice. They should spend five minutes on each.

3. Encourage students to take turns sharing their responses to the different questions in small groups. This gives the group several incidents to draw on as they read the novel. It helps students develop the skill of having a running dialogue with the story. After the small-group sharing, bring the class back together and ask: "Was everyone able to relate to at least one of the questions on the 'Have you ever?' " When all the students answer "yes," tell them that they all have something in common with the main character of their next novel.

FORMING STORY IMPRESSIONS

TIME ALLOTMENT:
One class period, plus homework

LEARNING OBJECTIVES:
• Anticipatory model (helping students compare their writing with that of the author as the novel unfolds)
• Improve interactive reading

MATERIALS:
• Pencil
• Paper
• Interesting chapter titles

Purpose

Using unusual chapter titles to form a story impression is a fun, creative writing exercise, as well as a great way to help students connect to the novel as they read. Students will continually check their story against the author's story.

Preparing the Activity

This assignment is best used with a novel that has unusual chapter titles. Here are the chapter titles from *The White Mountains* by John Christopher.

1 • **Capping Day**
2 • **"My Name is Ozymandias"**
3 • **The Road to the Sea**
4 • **Beanpole**
5 • **The City of the Ancients**

6 • **The Castle of the Red Tower**
7 • **The Tripod**
8 • **Flight and a Follower**
9 • **We Fight a Battle**
10 • **The White Mountains**

These chapter titles really give students something to think about and set their creative wheels in motion. You should type the chapter titles so that they will be ready to hand to the students, or you can put them on the overhead projector.

TIP

You can use the 'Have you ever?' questions as a test at the end of the novel. Students will explain how the main character of the novel related to each one of the questions. They can even pretend to be the main character and answer the questions from the character's perspective.

Doing the Activity

1. Post or distribute the chapter titles.

2. Ask students to write a creative story weaving all the chapter titles in order throughout their story. The chapter titles will be the basis for the students' stories.

3. The next day, ask students to share their stories with other members of their group.

4. Students will keep their stories in their literature logs so that they can refer to them as they read the novel. This should spark interactive reading as they check their story against that of the author's.

Story Impressions 4/14
(Table of Contents)

Today is Capping Day. Capping Day is the day when hunters go into the woods and try to shoot a deer. The hunter with the biggest deer receives the golden cap award.

My name is Darren and I am one of the hunters. I saw a big deer go into a cave, and I followed it in there. I searched everywhere, but I couldn't find the deer, so I walked out of the cave. The world seemed changed! The sky was purple, the trees had triangular, blue leaves, and the ground was white with black rocks.

I was walking around, when I saw another person. He was wearing something you would find in Romeo and Juliet. He told me his name was Ozymandias and that his world was in danger. The tripods were taking over the world, and they needed help to save it. I agreed to help Ozymandias find his friends and family, so they could attack the tripods.

They were on the road to the sea to get their weapons. After hours and hours of walking, they finally came to a beanpole. The pole was covered with a long, red bean plant and it was about 1,000 feet high. It was getting dark, so we decided to spend the night here, and early in the morning the next day, we would climb the beanpole.

I woke up at 6:30. Ozymandias was already up, and he had picked off fruit from trees for our breakfast. After breakfast, we started climbing the beanpole. It was about noon when we reached the top.

At the top of the beanpole, there was a little town called The City of the Ancients. We received our weapons there. When I asked Ozymandias why we couldn't just make weapons ourselves, he said that the people living in this city are the best in making weapons.

Now, we started walking toward the Castle of the

—2—

Red Tower. At the Red Tower, there lived Ozymandias's friend. He was a giant bird, and his name was Belutzinsa. We rode him around, looking for Ozymandias's friends and family. After a few days, we found everyone Ozymandia knew.

One day, when everyone was sleeping, a Tripod came walking through the forest. It was 3-legged, and it was made entirely out of metal. We were all scared because we weren't prepared to fight it, but luckily we rode Belutzinsa out of the forest.

We were heading toward the Black Demon Mountains. That was where the Tripods lived, and we were ready to fight them. Belutzinsa was soaring high in the sky, when we noticed someone was following us. It was another bird and it attacked us, but luckily, Belutzinsa was a better fighter and he killed the other bird.

It was in the afternoon when we reached the Black Demon Mountains. The Tripods were there and we attacked them. The battle went on for two weeks, finally we won.

Many people were killed, but at least Ozymandias and I were still alive. The next day, the Black Demon Mountains turned to a pure white. They looked as though they were frosted crystal. It was a beautiful sight. Ozymandias called them the White Mountains.

We had a big celebration that night, and the next morning I returned to the cave. I walked in and came back out. I was back to hunting.

JIGSAWING INFORMATION

TIME ALLOTMENT:
Two class periods

LEARNING OBJECTIVE:
• Building prior knowledge

MATERIALS:
• Maps, books, tapes, videos and other appropriate reference material on the given topic
• 5 different colors of construction paper
• Paper/pencil

Purpose

The jigsawing technique I learned at the California Literature Project is very helpful when you want to present historical and/or geographical information to your students. This technique creates some common prior knowledge before students read the book.

Jigsawing is a system in which children break into groups to do research on a particular topic. As experts in that area, students reorganize into other groups, and then teach classmates about their topic. They also learn from experts in other areas. Jigsawing is one way to put greater responsibility for learning on the students themselves.

For example, when I teach *The Cay*, I want my students to know about the geography of the Caribbean, general aspects of WW II, the U.S. role in WW II, Martin Luther King Jr., and prejudice in the 1940's. Instead of lecturing for five class periods on these subjects, I set up a jigsaw to get all the information to all my students in just two class periods. This method also helps students to be actively involved in their learning.

Preparing the Activity

1. Decide what background information students will need to know to help them understand the time period and geography of their upcoming novel and how many groups that will take. In my example from *The Cay*, I had five topics so I knew I would need five different groups.

It is important to give students power to make decisions about what they are learning whenever possible, but at this point in the assignment the teacher really needs to direct the topics as he/she is the person who is aware of possible gaps in the background information for the upcoming novel. If you are concerned about student choice, you may want to add that component later in this lesson during step #4.

2. Once you know your topics, gather books, tapes, videos, maps and other materials for each group so that they will have proper reference tools. You may want to have students gather the materials necessary to research their topic. If you choose to have the students take on this expanded role, you will probably find it necessary to give students an extra day for this task.

3. Make up specific task cards for each topic: assign one "expert" topic to each group, with each on a different topic.

For example, let's take one of my topics: the geography of the Caribbean and other parts of the world that relate to the novel. I made a task card for the "expert" group dealing with that topic so that I could guide their research. This also insures that every child in the "expert" group will learn and be able to report back about their topic. The task card should tell the group exactly what to do or answer. The group's task card might look like this:

By giving each group a task card, you are sure each group member will learn the proper information.

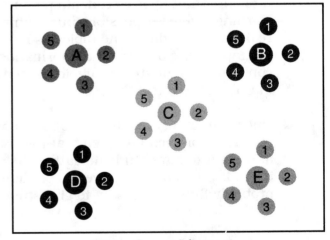

Draw a world map and locate the following:

- Venezuela
- Caracas
- Curaçao
- State of Virginia

- Holland
- Germany
- Aruba

4. Now that you have the materials together for the actual task, you can start preparing to set up your groups. The number of groups you have depends on the number of topics. We will continue with my example from *The Cay*. I have five different topics so I will need five different groups. I'm going to letter my groups A, B, C, D, E and give each a different color. Group A is red, B is green, C is blue, D is purple, and E is brown.

You will need to divide your class into the five different groups. Let's pretend I have twenty-five students in my class (wouldn't that be a dream come true?). Each group would have five members. Take your red construction paper and make five red cards numbered 1, 2, 3, 4, 5. Continue to do this with each color group. We will be calling the color groups (Group A, B, etc.) the Home Groups. We will call the number groups (1, 2, etc.) the Expert Groups.

Doing the Activity

1. As students come into the classroom, hand each one a card. Tell them to sit at the table that is displaying their color group (Home). You should have construction paper tents denoting where each color group should sit.

Home Group Diagram

2. Students are now seated with their Home Groups. Every child in the group should have the same color card with different numbers. Explain to the students that this is their Home Group. Tomorrow they will return to this group and be responsible for teaching the group a mini-lesson based on what they learn later today in their Expert Group.

3. Ask students to look at their color cards and notice the number on the card. The number on the card is the number of their Expert Group. At this point you should put new tents on the table displaying group numbers. Ask students to move to the table where their number is displayed. All number ones should be at the same table, all number twos at the same table, and so forth.

> **T I P**
>
> Organization is key. The color-coded cards really cut down confusion. I require students to keep their color-coded card with them for both days of the assignment.

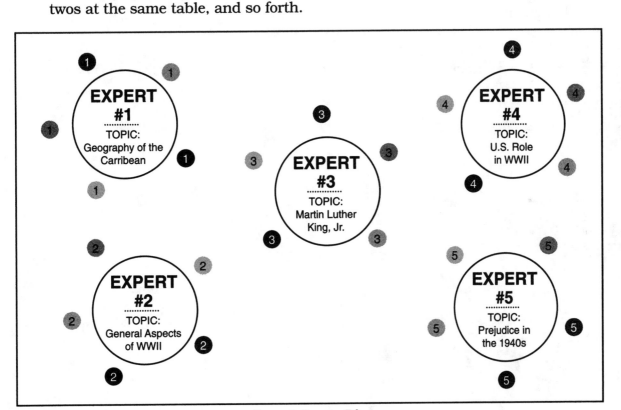

Expert Group Diagram

4. Students should spend the rest of the period completing their task card as a group. This is where students will use the reference material you have gathered. Each member will have a completed map or document with the appropriate information accurately completed. Each member of the group is responsible for bringing this information back to their Home Group tomorrow. Each member of the group must record his or her own information.

5. The following day, students meet back in their Home Group to share their information with those classmates. Students take turns reporting their information orally and visually. The students will take notes as the expert reports to the small group. Every student gets a turn to be the expert in their Home Group as each person researched a different topic. Each member of the Home Group should leave the group with written information on the five different topics. In order to make students accountable, I require them to have write-ups on each topic in their literature logs.

If your students do not fit nicely into five groups of five (mine never do), you may need to pair students up to do research. For example, one Home Group might have six students instead of five, but you still have only five topics. You could make two number ones in color group Red. The two number ones can help each other obtain topic information and report together to their Home Group. This is very helpful for students who are learning English as a Second Language.

"THROUGH" ACTIVITIES

KEY SENTENCES

TIME ALLOTMENT:
Three, five, or seven minutes

LEARNING OBJECTIVE:
• Main idea

MATERIALS:
• Two different colored sticky-note pads, such as yellow and pink
• Pencil
• Paper

Purpose

Key sentences is an easy homework exercise to help students focus on the main idea of a chapter. This homework assignment requires about 15 minutes of class time to discuss findings.

Preparing the Activity

Provide each student with two sticky-notes of different colors.

Doing the Activity

1. Ask students to read a chapter of their novel for homework. Have them look for two things in that chapter:

- **their favorite sentence**
- **the key sentence**

Students will use one sticky note (the yellow, for example) to mark their favorite sentence. As they are reading, they may find a stronger favorite sentence. All students have to do is move the sticky note to the new sentence. Students will use the second sticky note (the pink, for example) in the same way to indicate their key sentence.

2. Have students record their final favorite sentence and key sentence on a piece of paper. Students should also write a short explanation of the reasons for their choices.

3. As a small group, have students share their sentences and reasons for their selections. Have them decide on the "true" key sentence and why they think that is so. Share ideas with the larger group.

DOUBLE ENTRY JOURNAL

TIME ALLOTMENT:
Devote one class period to model the technique. The rest can be assigned as homework.

LEARNING OBJECTIVES:
• Critical thinking
• Note taking
• Interactive reading

MATERIALS:
• Pencil
• Paper

Purpose

Double entry journals help students take notes on the chapters they read and also help them react to what they are reading. Double entry journals are excellent for fiction as well as social studies and science selections.

Doing the Activity

1. Ask students to head their paper as follows:

   Chapter One

2. Post a large chart on the board. This will represent your journal. You will use it to model how to keep a double entry journal. Fold the paper in half. At the top of the left column, write **Notes, Facts**. On the right column, write **Quotes, Questions, Remarks**. Read chapter 1 with your students, and ask them to raise their hands when they come to an "important item." Write all the important items on the "Notes" side of your journal while students do the same in their journals.

Notes, Facts	Quotes, Questions, Remarks

As you continue to read aloud, model note taking. Write notes in the appropriate column. Encourage students to react actively to the novel as you read. Write remarks and questions in the appropriate column.

3. You may need to model this technique a few times. Thereafter, students should be able to write a double entry journal independently.

4. To keep interest high, assign a double entry journal for some chapters, but not all. (Many of my students elect to do a double entry journal on every chapter because it helps them comprehend the novel more easily, but I do not require this. They find that it is excellent study material for the end-of-the-novel test. I give students extra credit if they choose to do this on their own.)

Chapter 1

Notes/Facts	Quotes/Questions/Remarks
5 clocks in the village	Sounds like future, but what about villages?
Father owns only watch in village.	The watch is probably going to be significant.
Clockman checks clocks once a year, checks watch every 3 years	
Will takes his father's watch.	Disobeys parents
Intro. Jack Leeper	Cousin-Friend
Description of the setting. (pgs. 5-6)	Seems old, run down, poor.
Will is on his way to meet Jack and Henry jumps him	
Fight.	
Henry takes watch. Threatens to throw watch.	Bluffing
Jack breaks it up.	
Hint of Jack's Capping	What is Capping?

-5-

Chapter 1 (continued)

Vagrants	People whose Capping went wrong, They wonder
The Black Age?	Hints: man made ruins watch volts too many people, big cities
Tripods?	Give Capping big, 3 legged machines took over
Jack's Capping	Metal cap screwed onto their head control thoughts/actions become men/women age 14 ceremony
Jack and Will meet	Will is still questioning. Jack has changed and is controlled.

-6-

T I P

For my personal reading, I use a double entry journal whenever I read a new novel. It helps me to refresh my memory when I present that book in class. (In the "reactions" column, I also jot down possible activities I might use with students.) My personal journal also serves as a good model for my students.

WEBBING

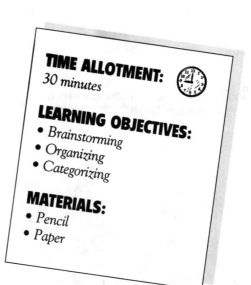
Purpose

Webbing (also called semantic mapping or clustering) is a great way for students to graphically organize and visualize material and to reinforce their knowledge of vocabulary words. Webbing can be used before and after reading and as a tool for preparing to study or write about a book.

Doing the Activity

1. My students have created webs about characters, relationships between characters, themes, and questions.

To help my students think of the characteristics of a character in their book, I place the character's name in the center of the board or chart. I ask students to suggest words or phrases they associate with the character, such as *mean, adventurous,* or *in love with neighbor.* I place those words around the main character's name, and we discuss students' responses.

My classes also enjoy using a web to talk about the relationships between characters, as you can see in the sample shown here.

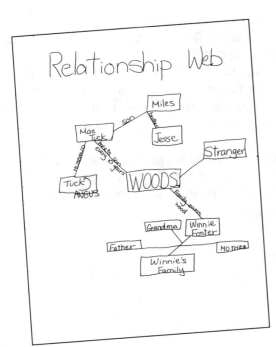

This child developed a relationship web for *Tuck Everlasting*.

2. Students can also create a web based on a key question related to the book, as shown here.

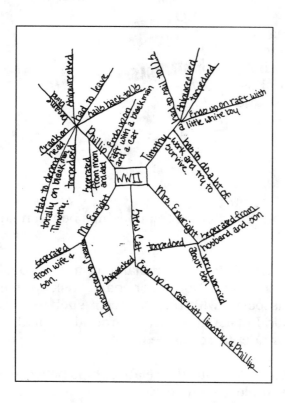

The prompt for this sample was "What were the effects of WW II on each character?"

3. Some students create a web and use it as the basis for organizing their thoughts for a formal paper with chapters. That is, they use the web as a kind of outline. For example, if a student read *After the Bomb*, by Gloria D. Miklowitz, they might place words in the center of the web as the title of the report (such as "The Atomic Bomb"). Each subtopic (such as "Effects on People in Story") becomes a chapter head. Then students follow the outline as they write the material for each chapter.

Once they have finished, students use the web again as a guide. They create a table of contents, listing the chapters in a desired order, and then place the text for each chapter in order. They finish the project by placing a cover on top and binding all the material together.

QUICKWRITES

TIME ALLOTMENT:
Three, five, or seven minutes

LEARNING OBJECTIVES:
• *Comprehension*
• *Running dialogue*
• *Active questioning*

MATERIALS:
• *Pen*
• *Paper*

Purpose

A quickwrite is a writing assignment in which you ask students to write quickly and for a short time on a topic you present.

Quickwrites get students to:

• **think generally about what they are reading**
• **make connections between characters (or events) in the book**
• **make connections between events in the book and those in their own lives.**

Quickwrites often last for between three to seven minutes. I often find that by having all students write, I get participation by every student, even the more retiring ones. When I rely on discussion only, the same few students sometimes dominate the discussion.

If you conduct quickwrites, I suggest that you focus on the content, not the mechanics, of students' work. Consider this a first draft—a rough work, not a final piece.

Doing the Activity

1. Ask students to write on a topic of your choice and tell them how long they have to complete the assignment. Do not interrupt them as they write.

2. Possible prompts might include:

• **How would you feel in the character's situation?**
• **What do you think will happen next?**
• **Based on the title of the book, what do you think the story is going to be about?**
• **What is the significance of this quote? (Take an interesting quote from the novel.)**
• **Compare two quotes from the novel (write both quotes on the board) and explain what this tells us about the character(s).**
• **Why do you think the author included this event in his/her novel?**
• **What would you do in the character's situation?**
• **What questions would you ask the author, and why?**
• **How would the main character fit into today's society?**

3. Ask several students to share their responses. This helps to generate a productive class discussion of the event or situation in the novel.

VENN DIAGRAMS

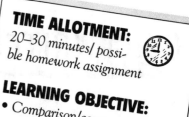

TIME ALLOTMENT:
20–30 minutes/ possible homework assignment

LEARNING OBJECTIVE:
• Comparison/contrast

MATERIALS:
• Pencil
• Paper

Purpose

Venn Diagrams are a great, visual way for students to compare and contrast information or characters. Venn Diagrams can be used to compare:

- **an individual character before and after an event in his or her life**
- **two different novels with the same theme**
- **a short story and a novel**
- **the student's life to that of the character in the novel**
- **the time period of the novel to present-day times.**

Doing the Activity

1. Ask students to create two large, overlapping circles and label each circle with the character's name (or the title of the story).

2. In the appropriate part of each circle, have students record statements about each character (or each story). The statements should be unique to that story or character. In the space shared by the two, have students record traits the characters have in common (features of the books that are shared). Discuss.

T I P

Some students find that Venn Diagrams are an excellent study aid. They help students to sort out facts, as well as analyze connections.

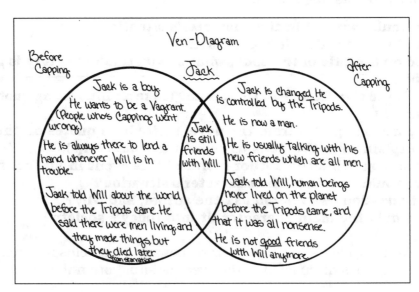

FILMSTRIPS

Purpose

Filmstrips help students to visualize scenes and to see the chapters as distinct scenes in sequence. They also help students to summarize the chapters.

Doing the Activity

Ask students to break down a chapter into its eight most significant details or events. In the filmstrip box, have them illustrate and write a small caption for each detail. The events must be in chronological order so that the filmstrip could run just as a film would. It must depict the chapter from start to finish.

You could also have students do a filmstrip for the entire book, instead of just a chapter. For that option, I suggest that you give the student several filmstrip worksheets.

TIME ALLOTMENT:
One class period, plus homework

LEARNING OBJECTIVES:
• Summarizing
• Sequencing

MATERIALS:
• Construction paper filmstrip (see sample below)
• White paper for illustrations inside the frames
• Markers or colored pencils

Julia enjoyed writing and drawing a filmstrip of the kidnapping scene for _The Vandemark Mummy_.

SHOW ME

TIME ALLOTMENT:
*30 minutes or home-
work*

LEARNING OBJECTIVE:
• *Visualization*

MATERIALS:
• *Paper*
• *Marking pens or colored pencils*

Purpose

With this project, students draw a scene based on the author's description. This helps students to visualize as they read.

Preparing the Activity

I prepare this assignment by taking authors' descriptions of settings from short stories and placing them on the overhead projector. As a class, we read the descriptions, highlighting the important parts. We do four or five of these, then I break the class into four or five groups. Each group receives one of the overheads and draws the scene based on the description. After about ten minutes, we come back together as a large group and compare the drawings to the descriptions and evaluate their accuracy.

Doing the Activity

1. Ask students to draw a setting from the book based on the author's description. Explain that students will be graded based on the details and accuracy of their work.

2. Share settings with the whole class, pointing out details. This will help develop students' abilities to visualize scenes as they read.

The student focused on many important details from *The White Mountains*, by John Christopher.

INTERIOR MONOLOGUES

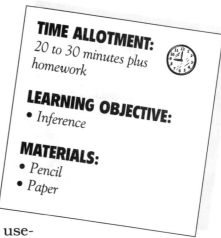

TIME ALLOTMENT:
20 to 30 minutes plus homework

LEARNING OBJECTIVE:
• Inference

MATERIALS:
• Pencil
• Paper

Purpose

In this activity, students are asked to deliver a monologue as if they are a character in the book. An interior monologue is a speech in which the character talks about his or her life, feelings, and/or experiences. The activity is useful because it helps students get "into" their character's thoughts. It also helps students make inferences.

Preparing the Activity

Talk to students about monologues. Point out, or ask students to point out, that a monologue is a speech in which a person thinks out loud without verbal response from others. A monologue may include a dialogue within one's self.

To make this clear, I always use the example of Jay Leno's monologue on *The Tonight Show* and am amazed at how many of my students watch the show and know exactly what I am talking about. Another show with a monologue your students may know is *Seinfeld*, the weekly television series.

After students have a clear idea of a monologue, we discuss the meaning of interior. I tie the two together so that students are sure of the meaning of interior monologue. For younger students, it may be easier to call this a thought bubble and use examples of comic strips where characters are thinking, rather than talking.

Doing the Activity

1. Focus on one event or turning point in the story. Make sure the character is faced with a moral dilemma or is in a situation where he/she might be questioning the status quo. Ask students to "become" the main character or a supporting character. Review the immediate prior events and ask students to write an interior monologue about how the character feels about the situation. Ask students to write in the first person ("I realized that . . . ").

It's helpful to distribute a large sheet of blank paper to make a thought bubble in which students write their interior monologue. Students can use binder paper underneath the blank paper as a line guide or simply draw in their own lines.

2. Encourage students to go beyond what they find in the book. Have them interpret how the character might feel.

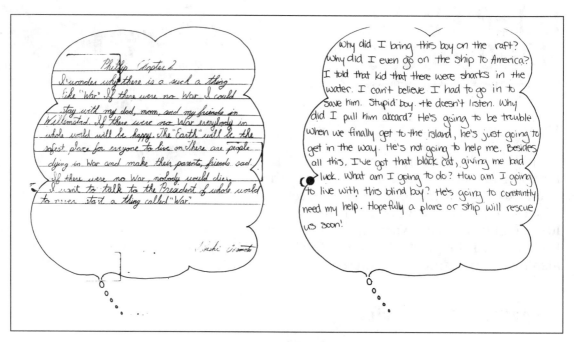

Interior monologues.

T I P

Need an idea for a great bulletin board? Invite students to draw their character on a sheet of paper and cut out the character. Draw the character's thought bubble on another piece of paper. Place the characters on one side and the thought bubbles on the other. Students have to match them correctly.

Two students who had finished *The Cay*, were asked to put themselves in the place of either Timothy or Phillip, just after the USS Hato had been blown up. I had them imagine that the two were left stranded on a raft together.

34

CHARACTER TRAIT POSTERS

TIME ALLOTMENT:
25 minutes to introduce the assignment and 1 or 2 class periods to create the poster

LEARNING OBJECTIVE:
• Character analysis

MATERIALS:
• Large white construction paper
• Crayons, colored pencils or markers

Purpose

Character trait posters are a fun, quick warm-up activity for getting students ready to do a character analysis paper. (See "Evaluation," on pages 61–72.) Students love to create their posters and enjoy diving back into their novel to obtain facts for the poster. The poster format also allows all students to share their ideas in a nonthreatening manner. Students know where and how to get information for their character analysis paper after this activity.

Preparing the Activity

1. Discuss with students the meaning of character traits. Include personality traits such as warm, nervous, and generous, and physical traits such as tall or blond.

2. Ask students to partner with a classmate and list some general, but positive, characteristics of that student. (See "Grouping" on page 10 for easy partnering ideas.)

3. Volunteer partners will share characteristics (for example, Jody is persistent, caring, and athletic).

4. Ask students to choose a main character from their novel for which they will create a character trait poster.

Doing the Activity

1. Invite students to draw a large picture of the character in the center of their paper.

2. Ask them to write quotes directly from their novel around the character's picture. This shows the character's different traits. In this way, students are discover character traits and learn how to back up their conclusions with evidence from the book. (See student samples on the following page.)

3. I ask students to supply:

- **2 quotes to show the character's personality**
- **2 quotes to show the wants/desires/ambitions of the character**
- **2 quotes to show relationships with other characters**
- **2 quotes to show how the character's speech relates to aspects of his or her personality**
- **2 quotes to show the character's appearance**

4. Students may label their categories or use symbols to designate categories.

5. Have students write an original paragraph analyzing the character.

Student samples.

TIP

Display character trait posters on a bulletin board so that all students can benefit from reading others' work. It will also help students gather ideas and possible approaches for their character analysis papers.

COMING-OF-AGE POSTERS

TIME ALLOTMENT:
Varies

LEARNING OBJECTIVE:
• Comprehension of a main theme

MATERIALS:
• Large construction paper
• Crayons, colored pencils or markers

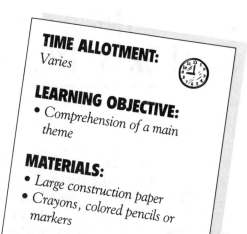

Purpose

This activity can be used with any novel that has a "Coming-of-Age" theme. Students reflect on the novel and analyze the events that led the character(s) to maturity.

Preparing the Activity

Students will pick out scenes from their novel that show the growth or maturity of their character as the novel progresses.

I begin by telling students about an experience in my own life that helped me to mature. I detail the incident from where I started ("I wouldn't share with my sister when I was ten"), the incident that changed me ("My sister was almost hurt in a car accident"), and where and how I ended up ("I realized how precious she is to me, and I was more willing to share with her").

I then ask students to work in pairs to talk about significant incidents in their own lives. (These experiences are shared only between partners as many of them are quite personal.) This exercise helps students to focus when they are given the assignment for the novel.

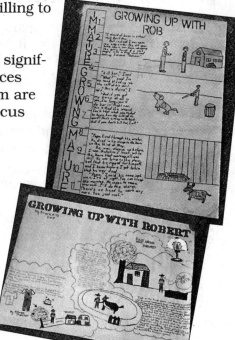

Doing the Activity

1. Students will find three separate passages throughout their novel that show the progression of the character's growth.

   • **Passage 1:** Where the character started.
   • **Passage 2:** An event that changed the character's life and led to maturity.
   • **Passage 3:** The final coming of age.

2. Have students divide their poster paper into three sections to represent the progression of the character. They are to copy the passage from the novel for each section and describe why they chose that particular passage and why they think it shows growth. They should also give a pictorial representation of each scene.

3. Students share their final products with the rest of the class. Since students inevitably choose different scenes, classmates will be reminded of all the events that actually led to the character's coming of age.

SCRIPTING FOR READER'S THEATER

TIME ALLOTMENT:
Four class periods

LEARNING OBJECTIVES:
• Comprehension
• Oral reading skills
• Review

MATERIALS:
• A children's story formatted into a reader's theater script (for demonstration purposes)
• Highlighter pens

Purpose

Reader's Theater is an interpretive reading activity in which students bring life to a text through the dramatic use of their voices and gestures. (Scripts are read aloud, not memorized.) Reader's Theater helps develop students' comprehension skills as well as oral reading skills.

Scripting takes Reader's Theater one step further. With Reader's Theater, I hand children a script, but with scripting, I ask students to create their own script. Scripting encourages students to get into their novel and analyze it deeply.

Preparing the Activity

1. From the library, find a short reader's theater script your students will enjoy (or write your own). Use it to demonstrate to your class what a script looks like and how to read from it. If you write one of your own, you may want to base it on a children's picture book.

I type the story on one sheet of paper and run off four copies: two for each of the two characters and two more, one for each narrator. I highlight the four different parts and give them to four students to practice.

2. The next day I ask the volunteers to perform the reader's theater for the class.

3. Then I place the original text of the story on an overhead projector. We discuss the story and the elements of reader's theater. Students learn that:

- for every speaker in a story there must be a narrator.
- good scripts come from stories or scenes that have a balance of narration and dialogue.
- you may delete something from the text, but you can never add to an author's writing.

4. As a group, we practice scripting the same piece the students have just demonstrated. First, students name the speakers and give them a symbol.

I like to use the story "Harriet" from *Tales for the Perfect Child* by Florence Parry Heide. It is a short, funny story about a whiner. It has a perfect balance of narration and dialogue, a key element for a reader's theater script.

5. On the overhead projector, we use symbols to indicate who should speak each line.

> **Harriet = H**
> **Mother = M**

(Next, students name the narrators and give them symbols.)

> **Harriet's narrator = N1**
> **Mother's narrator = N2**

Doing the Activity

1. Ask students to write a script of their own. Working in groups of four, they should choose an important scene from their novel, making sure it has a balance of dialogue and narration. Have each group choose a different scene.

2. Groups type their scene, then assign parts ("Beth, why don't you take the part of Christina?"). There is much valuable interaction between students as they decide which narrator will say what and the rationale behind their decisions.)

3. Students then choose their roles and highlight their parts.

4. Groups take turns performing their scenes. The students stand in front of the class, holding their scripts at waist level. The speakers stand in the middle with their narrators at their side.

N1: Harriet was a very good whiner. She practiced and practiced, and so of course she got better and better at it. Practice makes perfect.

N2: Some children hardly ever whine. Can you believe that? **N1** So of course they never get to be very good at it.

H: "Can I have a piece of that blueberry pie?" **N1** Harriet asked her mother while her mother was fixing dinner.

(excerpt from "Harriet" from *Tales for the Perfect Child* by Florence Parry Heide.)

CANDY BAR WRAPPER REBUS LETTER

TIME ALLOTMENT:
One class period

LEARNING OBJECTIVES:
- Comprehension
- Extending Ideas

MATERIALS:
- Empty candy bar wrappers
- Poster paper
- Marking pens
- Paper/pencil

Purpose

Students write letters pertaining to their novel, using empty candy bar wrappers as the "words" in a rebus. A rebus is a way of expressing words or phrases using pictures that represent the words or phrases. (If you are concerned about the junk-food aspect, consider using magazine ads ["Sale" or "Discount"] rather than candy wrappers.)

Preparing the Activity

Ask students to bring in lots of empty candy bar wrappers. (Duplicates are fine since groups will need the same wrappers or use a wrapper more than once in a letter.) Some of the most popular wrappers are:

NOW AND LATER	**LIFESAVERS**
CAREFREE	**WHOPPERS**
LOOK	**PAYDAY**
KISSES	**BAR NONE**
MOUNDS	**GOOD AND PLENTY**
BOUNTY	**BIG HUNK**
SNICKERS	**ROCKY ROAD**
U-NO	

Doing the Activity

1. Have students meet in groups of four to write a letter in rebus form. Possible formats include:

- **A letter to a friend about the novel**
- **A letter to a character in the book**
- **A letter from a character in the book**
- **A letter from one character to another character in the book**
- **A cover letter from a character requesting employment from a company**
- **A letter to parents**
- **A letter to the editor**

You can assign a particular format or give students a choice. I like to give students a choice, with the following requirements:

- **The letter must show a clear understanding of their novel.**
- **The letter must go beyond concrete facts.**
- **The letter must include as many candy bar wrappers (rebus) as possible.**

2. Ask students to write their letters on poster board, substituting the candy bar wrapper for words, thus making a rebus. The posters can then be displayed for the whole class to enjoy.

T I P

An excellent way to model how to write a "Candy Bar Letter" is to have the whole class create one together. I often start by having my class write a letter to their parents welcoming them to Back-to-School Night or Open House. Students work on their ideas in groups of four. Then we take the best out of each group's letter and compile it into a final letter. We put it on poster board, candy wrappers and all, and display it for the parents as they enter the classroom. Always a big hit!

POETRY

Purpose

Poetry is a terrific way for students to express their feelings about a novel or a character. Poetry helps students summarize the main points of the novel in a creative way. Poetry forms are easy to follow and give most students a feeling of success and pride. Products are so varied that displaying them will enhance your students' understanding of their novel.

TIME ALLOTMENT:
One class period

LEARNING OBJECTIVES:
• Synthesis of what students know about their character or novel.

MATERIALS:
• Construction paper
• Marking pens, crayons, or colored pencils

Doing the Activity

1. Offer students several different forms of poetry from which they can select to compose a poem about a character(s) in their novel or about the novel as a whole. Remind students these forms are suggestions and that they are welcome to find other forms of poetry with which to express themselves.

2. Invite students to write and illustrate the poems on construction paper. Display all poems on a bulletin board for class sharing.

FORM: DIAMANTE

Topic (noun)
Two describing words (adjectives)
Three action words ending in "ing"
Two words to capture topic—Two words to capture antonym
Three action words for ending noun
Two describing words for ending noun
Ending noun - Antonym

Example for *ONE-EYED CAT*

Healthy
Running, exploring
Chasing, killing, eating
Both eyes—One eye
Needs help, lonely, hurting
Limping, wailing
One-eyed

FORM: CINQUAIN
(used for characterization)

Noun
Adjective, adjective
verb-ing, verb-ing, verb-ing
four word free statement
synonym or equivalent for
the topic (noun)

Example for *ONE-EYED CAT*

Mr. Scully
generous, thoughtful
aging, nurturing, dying
a kind old man
senior

FORM: HAIKU
(used for setting)

5 syllables
7 syllables
5 syllables

Example for *ONE-EYED CAT*

A house in the hills
Placed in a quiet corner
With not a purpose

FORM: WHO-WHAT-WHERE-WHEN-WHY

Five phrases to answer the five W's.

Example for *TUCK EVERLASTING*

Winifred Foster Jackson
Dear wife, Dear mother
Treegap graveyard
1870-1948
Stayed on the wheel of life

FORM: ACROSTIC POEM

Example for *TUCK EVERLASTING*

W ater is in the wood she owns
I ndependent is what she wants to be
N eighbors think she is a hero
N ightgown was what Mae offered
I mage of Jesse made her heart almost stop
E verlasting Tucks tell her THE secret

F lapjacks is what she had at the Tucks
O dd is what the Tucks are
S he needs to decide whether to drink or not
T he Tucks are her friends
E lves is what her grandmother thinks about the music box
R unning away is what she did because she lost her patience

NOVEL SCAVENGER HUNT

TIME ALLOTMENT:
Two class periods: one to create the scavenger hunt questions/tasks for another group; the second to solve the scavenger hunt questions/tasks submitted by the other group

LEARNING OBJECTIVES:
- Review
- Questioning techniques

MATERIALS:
- Pencil
- Paper

Purpose

Novel scavenger hunts are created by students for students. First, they search the novel for great ideas for their scavenger hunt, then they search for answers to another group's scavenger hunt questions or tasks. This activity teaches students to go beyond questions like "What was the main characters' name?" or "Where does the story take place?" and ask questions that will make other students think about what they've read.

Doing the Activity

1. Working in groups of four, students are to create 15 challenging questions/tasks based on the novel, which will be part of a "scavenger hunt" the following day. Sample questions (from *A Day No Pigs Would Die*):

   - **How does Papa use a lesson from the *Book of Shaker* to help Rob in dealing with a dilemma in his life?**
   - **Would you rather have Mr. Tanner or Mr. Long for a neighbor? Why?**
   - **Even in their poverty the Peck family feels "rich." Why?**

2. Students do not have to put their questions/tasks in chronological order. Students should always ask for page numbers in the novel. This truly gives this task a scavenger hunt feel as the groups flip quickly through pages. (This really helps students remember large events in the book and the sequence in which they happened.)

3. The following day, students meet in their same groups. They receive a different group's scavenger hunt, and the fun begins. I give students 25 minutes to accurately answer as many scavenger hunt items as possible.

4. When time is up, students receive their original scavenger hunt back, as well as the answers from the other group. They correct each other's work.

5. The team with the most correct answers wins. I usually have bookmarkers or pencils on hand to give the winning group. I tell my class that they are all winners because they have just had a fast, fun two days of review for their upcoming test.

HOT SEAT

TIME ALLOTMENT:
15 minutes

LEARNING OBJECTIVE:
• Inference

MATERIALS:
• Pencil
• Paper

Purpose

This fun, fast-paced activity helps students understand the thoughts, feelings, and motivations of the main characters in their novel. With "Hot Seat," students answer questions as if they were actually a character from the book. "Hot Seat" forces students to go beyond the physical qualities of the characters. (I learned this activity while at the California Literature Project.)

Preparing the Activity

The day before you want to try this activity, invite students to write poignant questions for four characters from their novel as homework. You must choose the four characters so that all students are writing questions for the same characters.

Doing the Activity

1. Have students sit in groups of four. Students should number off, 1 through 4.

2. Show a chart designating a character (the same characters you assigned last night) for each number. (Example from Natalie Babbit's *Tuck Everlasting.)*

> **1 = Mae Tuck; 2 = Angus Tuck; 3 = Jesse Tuck; 4 = Winnie Foster**

3. Students are to "become" their character. They must answer questions from other members of the group as if they were actually that character.

4. Take turns putting each character on the "Hot Seat." When Mae Tuck is on the hot seat, for example, the other three students ask as many of their questions regarding Mae Tuck as they can in three minutes. Students can challenge the responses that "Mae Tuck" makes. The student must use examples from the book to prove that his/her answer is credible. After three minutes, ring a bell and put another character on the "Hot Seat."

T I P

You can model excellent questions by using students' examples from your first "Hot Seat" exercise or by simply role playing the difference between great and mediocre questions. (*Great:* If you truly feel that drinking from the spring of eternal life has made you feel like you are a "rock sitting beside the road," why would you ask Winnie to join you as your wife? If you truly love her, wouldn't you encourage her to lead a full and normal life? *Mediocre:* Why did you ask Winnie to marry you?)

STORY TRAILS

TIME ALLOTMENT:
15–20 minutes per chapter

LEARNING OBJECTIVES:
- *Comprehension*
- *Review*

MATERIALS:
- *Colored pencils or markers*
- *Construction paper*

Purpose

A story trail is a kind of time line of the major events of the story, displayed in a maze-like format. This activity helps students keep track of the story as it unfolds. It can be as simple as a picture and summary for each character, or it can turn into a metaphor of the whole novel.

Doing the Activity

Students will create a story trail for their novel. The simplest way to do this is to have students create a picture and short summary for each chapter. Students will do this all on one piece of large construction paper in a maze-like format.

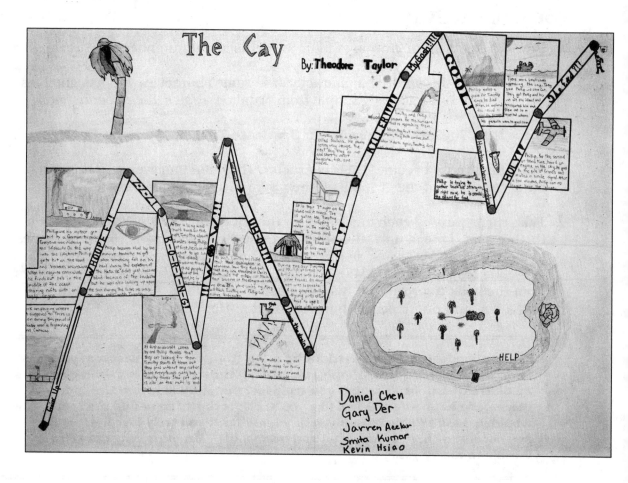

Along the way, they should add details to the trail that represent the story line. The fun and real learning begins when students get creative with their work. They can show peaks and valleys, depending on the action in the chapter. They can add rocky roads or clouds with silver linings. They can use an overall theme for their trail.

One of the best trails a student ever did for me was for *Tuck Everlasting*. Her whole story trail was in the shape of a Ferris wheel. Story trails serve as a good review of the book. They make excellent bulletin boards and help other students review as they look at each other's work.

GIFTS TO CHARACTERS

TIME ALLOTMENT:
20–30 minutes plus homework

LEARNING OBJECTIVES:
• Hypothesis
• Inference

MATERIALS:
• Student-drawn gift boxes (see sample below)
• Gift cards
• Markers, crayons or colored pencils

Purpose

Students are asked to give characters in their novel tangible or intangible gifts. The most important part of the activity is the card that is attached, which explains why the gift was given. Students are asked to take their knowledge of the character(s) and apply it to a gift-giving situation, as if the character is a dear friend.

Doing the Activity

1. Students will create three tangible or intangible gifts for the character(s) of their choice in the novel. Students can give three gifts to the same character or distribute the gifts to different characters. Students should be encouraged to think creatively, and give meaningful gifts.

2. Gifts are to be drawn inside the boxes, with a tag identifying which character is the recipient.

3. Students will attach a card to each gift. The cards must explain why the gift was given. For example, here is a card written to a character in *The Cay*:

TIP

You can have a gift exchange, allowing students to become the characters as they open "their" presents.

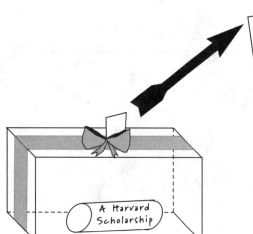

Dear Timothy:

My gift to you is a scholarship to Harvard University. Your thirst for knowledge is so great that I know you will make the best use of this gift. I know you were never given the opportunity to learn to read or write so I choose Harvard because it has the best teachers who will appreciate all the rich cultural and practical knowledge you have to offer them.

Happy Learning,
Justin
(6th grade student)

TABLEAU

TIME ALLOTMENT:
One hour

LEARNING OBJECTIVE:
• Inference

MATERIALS:
• Small index cards

Purpose

Tableau is a dramatic technique used to encourage students to put themselves in a character's "place." Students must be able to act out certain scenes and also infer what the character is thinking during a crucial scene.

Preparing the Activity

Select eight different poignant scenes from the novel. Describe each scene on index cards, one scene per card. Indicate what action the students should act out (see samples below from *The Vandemark Mummy*).

- **Mrs. Batchelor, the librarian, confronts Mr. Hall in front of the children on the library steps.**
- **Dr. Ken Simard corrects Althea at the mummy's unveiling.**
- **Althea and Phineas have a heart-to-heart talk about Mom.**
- **Phineas finds Althea tied up and in tears.**
- **The Halls confront Dr. Simard at the police station.**

TIP

Be sure students know ahead of time what they will be asked to do so they can convey emotions based on their understanding of the character. Demonstrate this technique before asking students to work independently. You may want to offer an alternative activity for students who feel uncomfortable acting in front of the class.

Doing the Activity

1. Distribute one index card to each group of students.

2. Have students decide how to act out the scene. Each member of the group must be a different character. (10 minutes)

3. Ask students to act out the scene and "freeze" at the climax.

4. Tap one student at a time to "unfreeze" him/her. The student must act and talk as his/her character. The "character" tells the audience how they feel at that particular moment. Tap the student at the appropriate time to "refreeze" the character. Then go on to another character.

5. Use the same process for each group, followed by a discussion of the group's interpretation of the scene and the characters' feelings.

CHARACTER "I HAVE A DREAM" SPEECHES

TIME ALLOTMENT:
Two to three periods

LEARNING OBJECTIVES:
• Critical thinking
• Speech writing/delivery

MATERIALS:
• Copies of Dr. King's speech or a video of the speech
• Pen/paper

Purpose

This activity requires students to take Martin Luther King, Jr.'s "I Have a Dream" speech as a model for a speech the main character in their novel will make. Students know that Dr. King's passion was for equal rights for all people, so they know their character's speech must revolve around the character's passion. This activity is best used for novels in which the main character(s) has a social or moral conscience.

Preparing the Activity

Show students a video of Dr. King's dynamic "I Have a Dream" speech. Then talk with the group about the specifics of Dr. King's dream. Discuss the content and the delivery.

Talk, too, about dreams students have for themselves, their families, their community, their environment, and their world. Once students have expressed themselves on these issues, it will be easier for them to place themselves in the character's shoes and think of the character's dream for his or her world.

Doing the Activity

1. Students are to assume the identity of the main character of their novel. Students are to pretend that the character has been commissioned to make a speech at _____ (students choose place depending on character). Students need to prepare a speech for the occasion. The speech they write can loosely fit the "I Have a Dream" structure. Encourage students to be original and innovative when thinking of what the impact will be on the audience.

2. Once students have written their speech, they must deliver the speech, in character, to the rest of the class. Discuss.

"BEYOND" ACTIVITIES

PAPER BAG REPORTS

TIME ALLOTMENT:
Students are given a week to complete this assignment for homework. (I always make sure my week includes a weekend.)

LEARNING OBJECTIVE:
• Review

MATERIALS:
• Lunch bag, one per student
• Crayons or markers
• Construction paper or other materials, such as clay
• Scissors
• Paste or glue

Purpose

Paper bag reports are a sure-fire way to get students excited about reviewing a novel. Invite students to draw a scene from the novel on the front of their lunch bag.

The strategy includes:

- **getting students to chose symbols that represent significant events or characters in the book**
- **understanding characters, setting, conflict and resolution.**

Students have such a good time with this assignment that they don't even realize they are reviewing for their final exam. In the five years that I have assigned the paper bag reports, I have yet to have a student neglect to complete the assignment. This statement is even more exciting when you realize that I assign this completely as a homework assignment. The only time spent in class on this assignment is when I explain the requirements. Students are highly motivated and excited about this project.

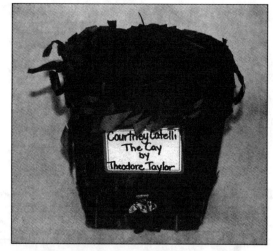

Preparing the Activity

On the front of the lunch bag, students draw a scene from the novel. They include the title of the novel, the author, and their own name.

On the back of the lunch bag students write the names of the main characters, and supporting characters, and write about the setting, conflict(s), and resolution(s) of the novel.

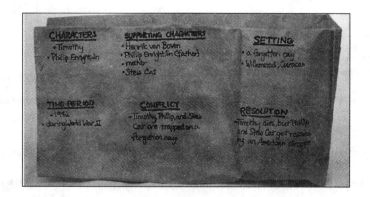

Inside the bag, students place at least eight objects that represent significant events in the novel or aspects of the characters' personalities. At least four of the objects must be handmade by the student.

Doing the Activity

When the students bring their bags to class, I have them share all aspects of their bags with their cooperative learning group. This helps students review the important scenes in the novel, as well as the main characters, supporting characters, setting, conflict, and resolution. Students have often commented on how helpful this was right before their test. Less able students reap the benefits of once again hearing and seeing the important aspects of the novel.

With sharing completed, I guide the class on a tour of all the other bags. This really boosts self-esteem and provides continued reinforcement of the important aspects of the novel.

The finished products make great classroom decorations. I have also found that our local children's librarian loves to display the projects.

NOVEL NEWSPAPERS

TIME ALLOTMENT:
Three class periods, plus homework

LEARNING OBJECTIVE:
• Thorough review of novel, including history of the time, character analysis, plot, subplot, and interpretation.

MATERIALS:
• Large newsprint
• Samples of newspapers
• Pens, markers
• Glue
• Scissors (if you are asking students to paste up)

Purpose

Novel newspapers are a great way to wrap up a novel study. Students will be using their knowledge of newspapers to create their own newspaper for their novel.

Preparing the Activity

1. Students may need a review of the parts of a newspaper.

2. Preparing a newspaper scavenger hunt is a fun way to review the newspaper. This is just a warm-up activity before students actually create a newspaper of their own. The activity will help to ensure that students are knowledgeable about the sections of a newspaper (on page 55). For example, your scavenger hunt may follow these guidelines.

> **Invite students to cut and paste a sample of each item listed below on a piece of paper:**
>
> • **Headline or banner:** the name of the newspaper
> • **Lead story:** the top news item
> • **Index:** a place to find out where in the newspaper all the stories are located
> • **Jump line:** line that tells the reader on what page the story continues
> • **Dateline:** location of the event, such as Detroit or East Orange
> • **Caption/cutline:** a brief explanation under a picture that explains what the photograph is about
> • **Editorial:** editor's opinion on various topics
> • **Feature story:** story of human interest
> • **Advice column:** such as "Dear Abby"
> • **Classified ad:** paid advertisement
> • **Movie guide:** movies with their schedules and theaters in which to see them
> • **Obituary:** information about person who died recently)

Doing the Activity

1. Place your students in groups of 4 to 6. I place my students in groups according to geographical location, so it will be easier for them to meet outside of

school. This assignment requires outside time! If that will not work for your students, then allow more class time for the assignment.

2. Groups will make an original newspaper for their novel. Everything about their paper will revolve around the time period, characters, and events of the novel.

3. Each group must include as many actual parts of a newspaper as possible in their novel newspaper.

Parts of the Newspaper

Advertisements
Arts and Entertainment
Business
Classified*
Comics
Daily living (advice, fashion, education)
Editorial*
Editorial cartoon
Features*

Front page*
Headline and lead story*
Letter to the Editor
Movie guide
Obituaries
Sports
Stock Market
Television
Weather

Parts of the newspaper that are marked with an asterisk are required for this assignment. A different member of the group must do at least one of the asterisked assignments. This insures that all individuals participate equally. Group members can do more than required by choosing some of the other options.

T I P

Evaluation of a group project is sometimes difficult. How do I know who did what? Here's how.

It helps if you require each student to do at least one hard news story plus one of the asterisked assignments (see page 55). At the end of the project, I ask the group to write me a letter detailing exactly what each student did in the group and how they got along. All students in the group must agree with the letter's contents and sign it.

I give each student an individual grade as well as a group grade. Students know this is part of their overall evaluation, so it usually makes for a smoother, more effective group environment.

4. Students must keep everything in their paper appropriate to the novel. Allow students some creative leeway. For example, a group of my students was doing a newspaper on *The Cay*, and one of the articles was about Donald Trump turning the cay into a multi-million dollar tourist attraction!

NOVEL GAME BOARDS

TIME ALLOTMENT:
One week

LEARNING OBJECTIVE:
• Review

MATERIALS:
• Tag board
• Construction paper
• Index cards
• Markers or colored pencils

Purpose

Students review the events and characters in a novel as they create a game based on the book. As they work, students become actively engaged, hardly realizing how much effort and understanding the project demands. This is a group project.

Students profit from game-making in at least two ways. First of all, as they work on their games and create challenging questions for others, students must have a thorough knowledge of the plot, the characterization, and the setting of their book. Second, students apply knowledge of their book as they play the games created by other groups. This provides an additional challenge.

Doing the Activity

1. Place students in groups of three or four. (I try to organize groups according to where they live, so they can meet after school.) If this is not possible, allow more time in the class to complete the assignment.

2. Explain that students are required to make up a game centered around their novel. Everything to do with the game, from the title to the design, should relate to the book. All games should include:

- **A detailed game board showing the turning points in the plot of the novel**
- **Question cards**
- **Rules/Directions**
- **All parts necessary to play the game**

The game must show students' understanding of the novel and be challenging.

3. Ask students to bring in games from home so that the class can discuss the components, the rules of play, and the overall strengths and weaknesses of each. As a group, develop a set of criteria for what makes a "good game"(the challenge? ease of understanding rules? fun? clear game board?). Armed with this knowledge, each group can plan and create a game of their own. Encourage students to design the game board, record the rules, and create the markers and other materials. Remind students to play their own games to work out the "quirks," and then make last minute revisions.

4. On official game-playing day, rotate groups so that students play all the games. I also ask students to evaluate the games based on the criteria developed earlier.

SYMBOLIC POSTERS/BOXES

TIME ALLOTMENT:
One class period, plus homework

LEARNING OBJECTIVE:
• Character analysis

MATERIALS:
• Poster paper or box (shoebox or gift-shirt size)
• Construction paper
• Library pockets or envelopes
• Paste or glue
• Marking pens, crayons or colored pencils
• Scissors

Purpose

With this activity, students create a poster or box in which symbols represent characters from their novel (such as a heart shape to represent a character who sacrifices for another). Symbolic posters/boxes engage students in a deep analysis of the main character(s) of the book.

Symbolic posters are assigned when:

• **students are investigating several characters in the novel**

Symbolic boxes are assigned when:

• **students are investigating one character in the novel.**

Doing the Activity

Ask students to make a poster centered on the characters in their novel. The poster must include the title, the author, sketches of the main characters, a summary of the novel, and symbols for the characters.

Point out that the symbols should tell us about a character's personality, wants or desires, looks, and role in the book. Symbols should be cut out of construction paper and attached to the poster in some fashion. (We place them in library pockets, along with the symbols. Students should write a brief explanation of what the sym-

bols mean for each character. Place explanations in the pockets, too.)
Symbolic boxes are done in much the same way, except that they represent only one character. The outside of the box should have the title and author of the novel. Inside the box, there should be a summary of the novel and symbols for the main character. There should also be a legend, explaining what each symbol has to do with the main character.

EVALUATION

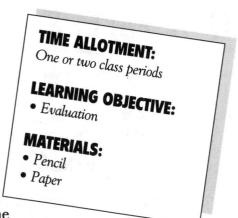

TIME ALLOTMENT:
One or two class periods

LEARNING OBJECTIVE:
• Evaluation

MATERIALS:
• Pencil
• Paper

Purpose

One of the most difficult decisions I make in teaching core literature is how to give a final evaluation of students' work. After students have spent so much time on intense, critical reading of the novel, a true/false quiz is not adequate and does not do justice to all the hard work the students have done. Students need their final evaluation tool to be as challenging and in-depth as was their study of the novel.

This and the following projects represent a variety of evaluation activities I've found effective with my students.

Essay Tests

I have found that an essay test is one of the most effective ways to measure students' mastery of a novel. The test allows students to take what they know about the novel and develop the ideas more critically, applying it to different situations.

Essay tests can consist of five or six questions based on the different themes of the novel, such as "Family" or "Friendship". It should take students one or two class periods to take the test. I always allow students to use their books and their literature logs to answer the questions. Obviously, the questions must be challenging and go beyond literal comprehension if the students are to be challenged.

If I were to develop essay questions for *Island of the Blue Dolphins*, for example, I would make a list of the themes of the book: survival, overcoming prejudice, death, determination, and women in nontraditional roles. then I'd create at least one question per theme.

FINAL PAPERS

An alternative to the essay test could be to write a final paper on the novel. The paper can be centered on a theme (such as Death) or a character (such as Charlotte).

Stages of Preparing a Character Analysis Paper

Here is the format I use to help structure my students' work.

Prewriting

1. Hold small group discussion about the novel.

2. Ask students to create semantic maps and jot down notes on each character. Share these with the large group. (Chart it so students get more ideas.)

3. Ask students to do two quickwrites on the characters. (Students may choose two different characters or two aspects of one character.) Share with partners.

4. Discuss the form of the paper. (How do you want to say it?)

- **Essay**   • **Interior Monologue**
- **Poem**   • **Dialogue**

5. Give questions to help focus writing.

- **What do you want to say about your character?**
- **Why does it seem important to say this?**
- **To whom are you speaking?**
- **How do you want to say it? (form)**

Writing

6. Begin writing first draft. (Use evidence from the novel to support statements.)

7. Finish first draft.

Revising

8. Conduct reader/writer workshops (done in trios).

- **Students in the trio read each others' papers silently and record responses on paper.**

• **Responders answer these questions:**

What is the writer trying to say?
Do students have evidence from the novel to back up what they are trying to say?
Is the paper clear?
What would you like to know more about?
What rubric score would you give the paper and why?

WRITING RUBRIC

6-EXCEPTIONAL WRITING

-Strong sense of voice
-Writer uses full sensory description("showing" writing)
-Similes/metaphors are used
-Dialogue is used naturally and adds to the piece
-Organization is smooth
-Excellent vocabulary is used
-Mechanics/spelling are very correct

5-STRONG WRITING

-Interesting and easy to read
-"Showing" writing is used
-Similes/metaphors are used
-Dialogue is used correctly
-Organization of the paper is good
-No breaks in the flow
-Good vocabulary is used
-Mechanics and spelling are strong

4-CAPABLE WRITING

-Writing is good
-Some "showing" writing is used but there are places where "telling" writing is used
-Dialogue is used and is usually correct
-Organization is acceptable
-Some breaks in the flow (not serious)
-Grade-level vocabulary is used
-Mechanics/spelling are at grade level

3-DEVELOPING WRITING

-Writing is predictable
-More "telling" writing is used than "showing" writing
-Some dialogue is used but frequently indirect
-There are breaks in the flow but the essay is still readable
-Simple vocabulary is used
-Mechanics/spelling are noticeably incorrect

2-LIMITED WRITING

-Writing is sketchy and brief
-A great deal of "and then" writing
-Little dialogue is used
-There are great gaps in the essay and it is difficult to follow
-Vocabulary is simplistic
-Mechanics/spelling are poor and interfere with readability

1-EMERGENCY WRITING

-Writer is just learning and will need individual attention.

9. Discuss papers and responses in trios.

10. Revise the first draft based on feedback.

11. Publish

This form can be slightly altered for a theme paper, if you wish.

CHOICE ESSAYS

Another final project is to give students many writing prompts based on your novel and allow them to choose one. This way you can assign aspects of the book that might require extra research, and the assignment can be done for homework. I usually assign the choice essays on a Tuesday and have them due the following Tuesday. This gives students time over the weekend also.

Sample choice essay topics from
The Summer of the Monkeys

1. You are a boy or a girl in rural Oklahoma. You live in the foothills of the Ozark Mountains, in the heart of Cherokee Nation. Research life there around the late 1800's. Write a Sunday Supplement for the newspaper on what your life was like then. **(Report of Information)**

2. Imagine that Jay Berry did not decide to give his parents the reward money so that Daisy could have her operation. How might Grandpa have responded to Jay Berry and how might the story have been different? **(Analysis/Speculation)**

3. Write an essay for the "My favorite character contest." Convince readers of why the character you picked is your favorite. Briefly describe the character. Give reasons why you like the character more than other characters. **(Evaluation)**

4. Papa and Jay Berry were left alone to fend for themselves when Mama took Daisy to the hospital. Pretend that you are Papa and write a letter to Mama describing Jay Berry's first attempt at cooking dinner. **(Eyewitness memoir)**

5. Your job is to try to catch Jimbo. What methods will you use? How would you get the other monkeys on your side? What will you do with him if you catch him? Prepare a plan. Anticipate problems. **(Problem/Solution)**

6. Wilson Rawls ends the story saying that he believes in the fairy ring and still looks for it. Write a story about Wilson's adventure in trying to find that fairy ring. Will he find it? What problems will he have? What will he wish for? How does he feel? **(Story)**

7. Choose a character in the story and take notes about the character (physical appearance, emotions, personality, major events in his/her life, friends, interests) as you read. Use incidents from the story to show what the character is like as you write an account of your character for the book *Who's Who Book in Oklahoma*. **(Firsthand Biographical Sketch)**

AUTHOR PROJECTS

TIME ALLOTMENT:
The project is spread out over a four month period. Actual class time is approximately 10 class periods.

LEARNING OBJECTIVE:
• Develop interest in different authors and genres

MATERIALS:
• Multiple books by many authors
• Poster board
• Markers, crayons, paints
• Envelopes and stamps

Purpose

The Author Project encourages students to conduct an in-depth study of one writer. Students read several different works by that author. (The authors are chosen based on students' interests.) The project evolves over a four-month period so that students can write to their author (if he or she is living). This project allows plenty of time for students to read and discuss the author's works before making their final presentation.

Preparing the Activity

1. You will need to collect many works of several different authors. Try to have a large selection of authors to choose from. You will need to be familiar with the writers so you can give students an "author" talk on each to spark students' interest.

Some authors my students have liked in the past are:

AVI

LOIS DUNCAN

LOIS LOWRY

JOAN LOWRY NIXON

SCOTT O'DELL

KATHERINE PATERSON

GARY PAULSEN

ZILPHA KEATLY SNYDER

MILDRED TAYLOR

THEODORE TAYLOR

LAURENCE YEP

JANE YOLEN

2. In order to help students make a more informed choice about which author to choose for their project, give students a short talk about each author and mention the type of books he or she writes. Students should take notes. Make students aware that they will get one of these authors for a project on that requires reading his or her works. They should be listening for authors who appeal to their interests.

For homework that night, ask students to write a letter to you detailing, in order of preference, the three authors they would most like to read.

Place students in groups according to that interest. (If too many students want the same author, I award first choices based on the quality of the students' letters. The best letters get their first choices.) A good size for group is three to four students.

3. Distribute an author's books to each group. Encourage students in the group to each read a different title by their author. When they make their final presentation on their author and his/her books, they will thus have a variety of titles to share.

4. Approximately one month later, ask students to write a letter to their author or request information from the author's publisher. The letter should include mention to how they feel about the author's work; a request for a biographical statement; and, possibly, for a picture. Be sure to include a self-addressed stamped envelope for the author or publisher to respond. This is very important and, in my opionion, doubles the odds of getting a response.

Doing the Activity

1. About six weeks later, you are actually ready to begin the project assignment. By this time students have had ample time to read their author's works. Students will be required to create a display for the library about their author. (Our local library is wonderful about displaying students' work.)

2. The display must be colorful, artistic, and accurate. It must prominently display the author's name and include the following elements:

- **A biography of the author**
- **A list of other books written by the author**
- **A summary, evaluation, and visual for each book read by the group.**

Summaries must be varied for each book. Students may choose to do their summaries in any of the following formats:

- **Letter**
- **Newspaper front page**
- **Diary entry**
- **Film strip/comic strip**
- **Interior monologue**
- **Persona**
- **Mini-ABC book**
- **Poem**
- **Mini-game board**

3. Allow students approximately five class periods to create their display. They will probably have to tape several pieces of poster board together to hold their project.

4. Have students share their author projects with the rest of the class. Hopefully, this will spark interest in other authors.

5. Ask your local or school library to display the author projects for you.

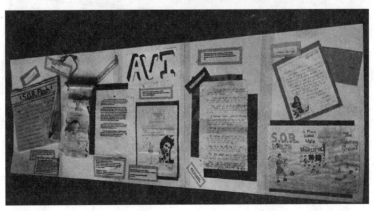

ABC LEARNING DOCUMENT—A YEAR OF BOOKS IN REVIEW

TIME ALLOTMENT:
2 weeks

LEARNING OBJECTIVES:
- *Review*
- *Evaluation*

MATERIALS:
- *Paper*
- *Marking pens or colored pencils*
- *Binding materials or folders*

Purpose

Students create a large class book (organized alphabetically) in which they review, summarize, and evaluate the novels they have read during the school year. We call the final product a learning document because anyone who reads the book can "learn" something about the books reviewed. This encourages students to write detailed or thoughtful reviews.

Doing the Activity

1. Explain that students will make an ABC book based on all the books they've read or enjoyed that year. Have them assemble 26 sheets of paper and add a cover. Work with the loose sheets until the end of the project, when they will be bound.

Write a letter of the alphabet on each page. Each letter will have the title of a different novel, a picture of a scene from the novel, and a summary with evaluation of the book.

Students will need some leeway on some of the letters like *Q*, *X*, or *Z*. For example, they can write "X-citing suspense stories" for *X*. If a student has not read or listened to 26 books during the year, I allow some of their pages to center around aspects of reading, such as *I* is for important characters.

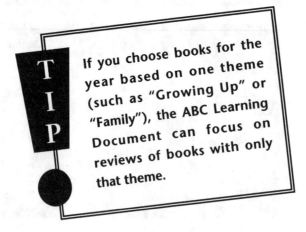

T I P

If you choose books for the year based on one theme (such as "Growing Up" or "Family"), the ABC Learning Document can focus on reviews of books with only that theme.

A = *A Day No Pigs Would Die*

B = *Beauty*

C = *The Cay*

D = *Don't Look Behind You*

E = *Tuck Everlasting*

F = *Face on the Milk Carton*

G = *Gold Cadillac*

H = cliff *Hangers*

I = *Island on Bird Street*

J = *Jolly Postman Christmas Delivery*

K = Killer novels

L = *Locked in Time*

M = Mysteries

N = *Night Swimmers*

O = *Other Side of Dark*

P = *Pigman*

Q = Quality not quantity

R = *Wolf Rider*

S = Suspense novels

T = *The Witch of Blackbird Pond*

U = Unidentified characters

V = *Vandemark Mummy*

W = *White Mountains*

X = X-citing chapters

Y = Young Adult Novels

Z = Zillions of Great Books

T I P

ABC Documents can be a great way to review all the topics across the curriculum for an entire year— not just literature.

2. Have students bind their finished products and share with the class. Use the bound books to motivate your next-year's students. The new students can get excited about upcoming books they might read soon.

NOTES

NOTES